EARLY LEARNING EXPERIENCES IN SCIENCE

Carmen Montemayor

by Imogene Forte and Joy MacKenzie

Incentive Publications, Inc.
Nashville, Tennessee

Illustrated by Gayle Seaberg Harvey
Cover Design by Marta Drayton
Edited by Leslie Britt

ISBN 0-86530-293-6

PRINTED IN THE UNITED STATES OF AMERICA

Table Of Contents

You Can Be An Earth And Sky Scientist!

You Can Be A Laboratory Scientist!

You Can Be A Science Detective!

About This Book . . .

Early Learning Experiences in Science has been planned to help young children learn through experimentation, through creative involvement in directed activities, and finally, through the joy of discovery.

Young children are curious about and extremely sensitive to their environment. They instinctively push and pull, take apart and attempt to put together again, smell, taste, feel, and listen to things around them. "Why?" "What?" "When?" "Where?" and "How?" are words they use naturally and often. It is this interaction with their environment that parents and teachers can either nurture and encourage or inhibit and retard. Children who have had many happy, satisfying opportunities to use their hands, feet, eyes, ears, and whole bodies are much more apt to adjust happily and successfully to more structured learning experiences.

The purpose of the activities in *Early Learning Experiences in Science* is to help children acquire and make meaningful use of beginning science skills and to sort out and bring into focus scattered knowledge and isolated concepts.

The book includes a mix of hands-on experimentation, directed pencil-and-paper activities, and discussion activities. While instructions are directed to the child, an adult will, of course, need to read and interact with the child in the interpretation and completion of the activities. Ideally, the projects will be presented in a stress-free setting that will afford time for the child to question, explore, wonder, and ponder—and to develop an abiding, imaginatively inquisitive approach to science skills and concepts. The fanciful illustrations will provide added incentive for lively science interaction. Each activity is intended to contribute to the development of a sound foundation upon which the basic skills necessary for school readiness may be built. They have also been planned to provide a flexibility and freedom to enhance the child's growth in science and related areas, environmental awareness, and creative self-expression.

You Can Be A Scientist!

You can be . . .

. . . a backyard scientist.

. . . a bathtub scientist.

. . . a library scientist.

. . . a puddle scientist.

. . . a kitchen scientist.

. . . a windowsill scientist.

. . . or any kind of scientist you wish to be!

. . . a sidewalk scientist.

9

Tools For Science

Scientists often needs tools to do their work.

Ask a grown-up to help you gather some of these things and put them in a big dishpan or pail so that they will be ready when you need them.

Don't forget to put your science equipment away neatly when a project is finished!

YOU CAN BE A PLANT SCIENTIST!

A plant scientist learns about growing things.

A BEAN RACE

Plant several bean seeds in each of two small containers.

Place one in a sunny spot.
Put the other in a dark corner or closet.
Give them a little water each day.

Which pot of beans grows fastest?
Can you guess why?

Plants need AIR, WATER, and LIGHT to grow.

After awhile, move the pot you put in the dark to a light place. See what happens —You guessed it!

12

About Seeds . . .

Seeds travel from one place to another in lots of interesting ways.

Color the pictures that show these ways:
- Seeds can blow in the wind.
- Animals can carry seeds on their fur.
- Birds can carry seeds in their beaks.
- People carry them many ways.

My Name Is _____

A Matching Game

Can you draw a line from each plant to the kind of seeds it produces?

My Name Is _____

Make A Seed Poster

You will need seeds, a big sheet of paper, and some glue.

See how many kinds of seeds you can find.
Glue the seeds on the paper and hang the paper on a wall or door.

Ask your friends and family to help you identify the seeds.

Seed Surprise!

Here is a body poem for you to enjoy.

Seed so tiny, underground. *(Roll body in a tight ball, on the ground.)*

Raindrops gently falling down. *(Wiggle fingers over head.)*

First a shoot, *(Shoot one arm upward.)*

Then a bud. *(Put second arm over head.)*

A flower BURSTS up from the mud! *(Stand and spread arms over head in a circular motion.)*

A Perfect Posy

You will need crayons, scissors, paste, and some string or yarn.

Most plants have four parts:

FLOWER or FRUIT

LEAVES

STEM

ROOTS

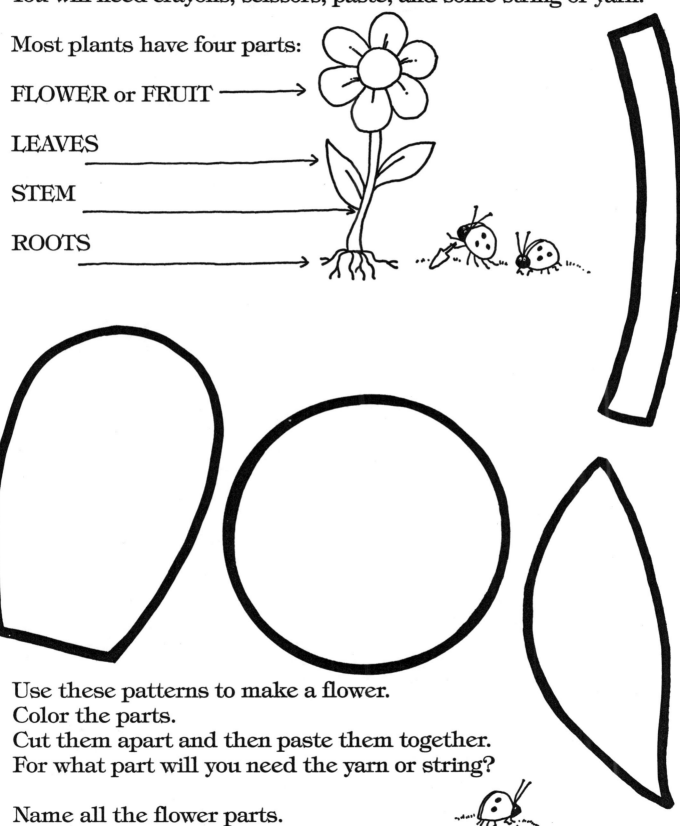

Use these patterns to make a flower.
Color the parts.
Cut them apart and then paste them together.
For what part will you need the yarn or string?

Name all the flower parts.

Bag A "Real-Live" Monster!

Put a potato in a bag.
Hide it in a dark place for
a few weeks.

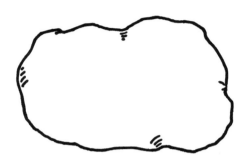

Take a peek now and then
to see how your monster
is growing.
Count the days the
monster is in the bag.

After a few weeks,
let him out.
Use a marker to give him
eyes, a nose, and a
ferocious mouth.

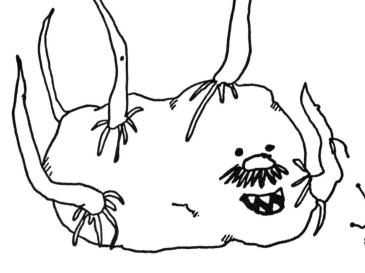

Scare your friends with the
monster!

Grow A Garden On Your Windowsill

Plant parsley seeds on a damp sponge and you'll have a funny-looking sponge with green "hair," and plenty of parsley to eat.

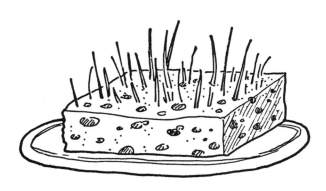

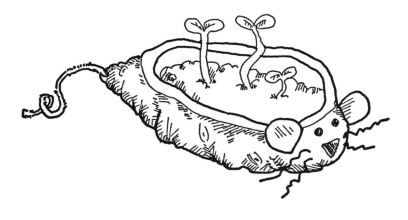

Make a potato planter for a friend.
Cut a large potato in half, scoop out the middle, and plant some grass or bean seeds. You could add pipe cleaners, buttons, and bows to give your planter a personality!

Put carrot tops in a shallow bowl of water and wait for the green, lacy sprouts to appear.

If you rest a sweet potato on toothpicks in a jar of water, you will soon have a lovely trailing vine to fill your windowsill.

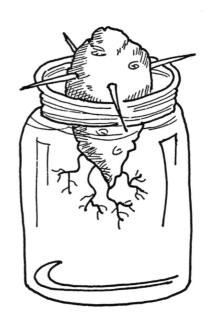

Place dry lima beans on a bed of damp cotton. Place the cotton on top of a glass of water. PRESTO—CHANGE—O! It won't be long before you see sassy bean sprouts!

Invite some friends to see your garden, and tell them all about how it grew!

Some Plants Are To Eat

Use pictures cut from magazines OR draw your own pictures to illustrate each page.

Cut on the solid lines and fold on the dotted lines to make a book about plants you can eat.
(Be sure the page numbers are in order!)

I sure am glad there's a peanut plant!

PEANUT BUTTER

JAM

Bread begins with grains of wheat . . .

. . . aren't made by little creatures on the Milky Way or Mars.

2   11

Throw away this part.

But most of the tastes
You've learned to love
Were plants not long ago.
Plants' seeds and leaves
And fruits and flowers
Make many foods we know!

HOWEVER . . .

Never eat a plant
you don't know!
Some plants are poison!

12

22

Name_____

SOME PLANTS
ARE TO EAT

Did you know that . . .

1

Berries, grapes, and oranges . . .

4

. . . like rye and sesame?

9

Beans are ground for coffee?

Leaves are soaked for tea?

The mint and fruity flavors of
gum and candy bars . . .

10

. . . and cakes from corn
are made?

3

And lots of seeds make
tasty treats . . .

8

. . . are what's in marmalade?

24

5

YOU CAN BE AN ANIMAL SCIENTIST!

An animal scientist observes living creatures.

THE HOME OF MY ANTS . . .

Put several inches of sand or soil in a large jar or aquarium.
Add about six ounces of water, some ants, and some food scraps.
Add a piece of cotton.
Keep the cotton damp by adding 6 or 8 drops of water to it each day.
Watch your ants live and work.

(Provide meals of tiny food crumbs, specks of hamburger, a drop of honey on a crumb, or a crumb soaked in sugar water.)

Fall In Love With A Bug!

Carefully catch an insect and put it in a jar.
Put the top on tightly, and punch some holes for air.

Ask a friend to observe the insect with you.
See if you can each tell **3** things about the insect.

You will want to tell about . . .
- the insect's size, shape, and color.
- how many legs it has.
- what other body parts it has.
- how it moves.

Find the one that is NOT an insect.
Draw a box around it.
Color the insects.

Did you remember to count the legs?

My Name Is _____

Ladybug Mine

Color and cut out the ladybug body and wings.
Paste the wings over the body as shown.
Bend pipe cleaners to make curly antennae and glue them
to the head.
Cut another pipe cleaner into six parts and attach for legs.

When your ladybug is finished, ask a grown-up to read the
poem and imagine together the secrets that Ladybug
might tell.

Glue wings on dots

What does a
ladybug do all day?
Just flit through the grasses
And eat and play?
Where does she come from?
Just where does she go?
Is she really a lady?
How can you know
If she sleeps or takes baths?
How does she talk?
How far on those tiny, six legs
Can she walk?

Ladybug, Ladybug,
whisper to me.
Tell me your secrets . . .
I'll keep them . . .
You'll see!

Sometimes
a Ladybug is
called
"Ladybird" or
"Lady beetle."

Bug-A-Boo!

Help these bugs and spiders find their homes!

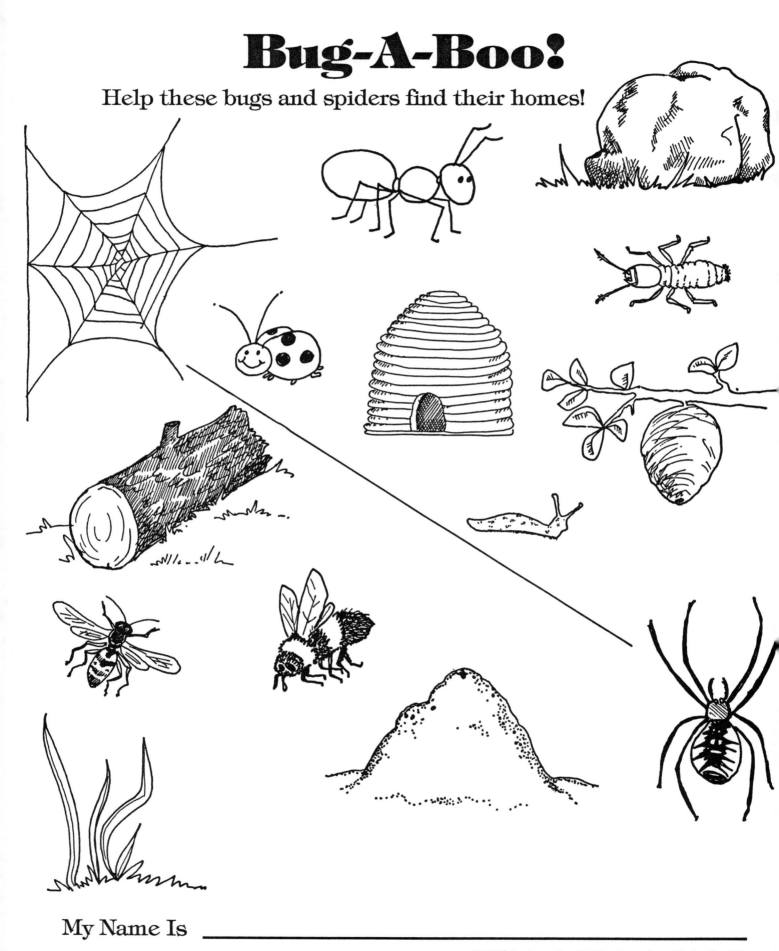

My Name Is _____

28

Put A Hoptoad In Your Pocket!

Put each animal in the correct pocket.

animals
that
walk

animals
that
swim

animals
that
crawl

animals
that
hop

animals
that
fly

Color the animals that can go in two or more pockets.

My Name Is _____

Can You Tell A Tale?

Match the heads and tails.

My Name Is _____

Jungle Search

Search the jungle to see how many creatures you can find.
Then color them.

Did you find these animals?

| Monkey | Giraffe | Zebra | Hippo | Lion |
| Rhino | Bird (Toucan) | Elephant | Turtle | |

Critter Cages

Here are some good ideas for making critter cages.

Critter cages are only for keeping animals so that you can observe them for a brief time.

Don't forget to let your critter go free after you've watched for a while.

Recipe For A Happy Tummy

Color, cut, and paste pictures to set this table with lots of healthy things to eat!

My Name Is _____

. . . for cutting and pasting!

Which foods are not good for you to eat all of the time?

Recipe For A Tummy Ache

What might be making this person feel so bad?
Perhaps he hasn't been eating healthy foods.
Draw and color pictures of unhealthy foods on his
stomach to show what might have made him feel sick.

My Name Is _____

Look What A Body Can Do!

(Chant this body poem or sing it to the tune of
"Skip To My Lou.")

Clap my hands,
One-two-three.
Stomp my feet,
Hard as can be.
Blink just ONE eye,
Then blink TWO.
Look what a body can do!

Knock my knee bones,
Tap my toes.
Shake my head and
Touch my nose.
Reach up to
The sky so blue.
Look what a body can do!

Rub my tummy.
Twirl around.
Sit my fanny
On the ground.
Cover my mouth and
Say, "ACHOO!"
Look what a body can do!

See How You Grow!

- Copy the parts of the growing chart.
  (Copy as many middle sections as you need to make your chart taller than you are.)

- Cut along the outside edges.

- Place the part with the rabbit at the bottom.
  Place the part with the giraffe at the top.
  Put the plain parts in between.

- Tape the parts together and ask a tall person to help you attach it to a wall or door.

- Stand tall beside your chart and ask someone to mark your height and the date.

- Mark your height every few weeks.
  See how you grow!

38

See How I Grow!

39

Mix-Up, Fix-Up

What a mixed-up world this is!
Almost everything is in the wrong place.

Cut on the dotted line around each animal.
Paste each one in its proper place on the next page.

My Name Is _____

Living Things

All living things need air, water, and food to stay alive.

POP

How many living things can you find on this page?

Touch each one as you say its name.

ICE COLD POP

POPCORN

Can you find at least 6 non-living things that begin with the letter 'P'?

YOU CAN BE AN EARTH AND SKY SCIENTIST!

An earth and sky scientist explores the natural world.

EYE SPYGLASS

Here's a wonderful new way to explore your natural world—a little piece at a time.

Cut the bottom from a large plastic bleach or milk jug. Wash it well. Hold the small end to one eye and close the other eye so that you can see out the large end of the bottle.

Now try the other end.
Press your face against the large open end of the jug.
Keep both eyes open.
You can see only a small piece of world.
Choose a piece of earth or sky to observe quietly.
Hold your spyglass very still for a few minutes.
What colors do you see?
What shapes do you see?
Can you see anything moving?
Which end of your spyglass do you enjoy most?

I need an elf-size spyglass!

Go Trailblazing

Explore the outdoor world by making a crooked trail for someone to follow.

You can do this by leaving markers at short distances along the way . . .

. . . OR by making a popcorn or seed trail.

Make your adventure safe for children and animals, and be careful not to damage the environment.

Remember to clean up any mess you make!

The Season's The Reason

When the part of the earth where you live leans toward the sun, and the weather gets very warm, it is SUMMER.

When the earth leans away from the sun, and the weather turns cold, it is WINTER.

In between WINTER and SUMMER are SPRING and FALL. We call these the SEASONS.

SPRING

WINTER

SUMMER

FALL

Use your crayons, or colored paper scraps and glue, to show how a tree might look during each season of the year.

Cut apart each tree. Then fold each tree in half lengthwise so that you can display your tree picture.

46

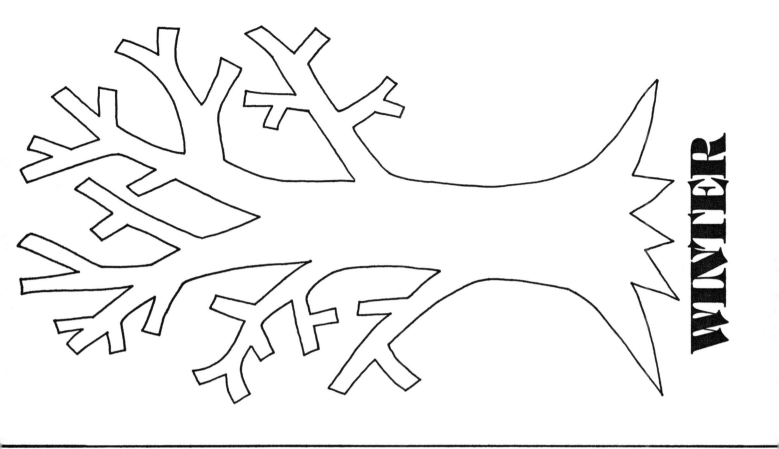

WINTER

FALL

SUMMER

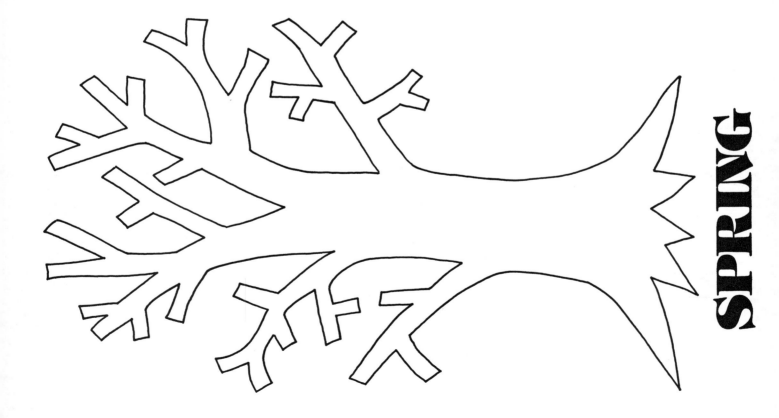

SPRING

Peek-A-Boo Bedrooms

Cut VERY CAREFULLY along just the dotted lines of this page.
You will be making some tiny windows in the picture.

My Name Is _____

49

Put glue or paste along the outside edges of the second page.
Lay the first page EXACTLY on the second page.
Now you can peek through the windows at some creatures who hide underground in winter.
Can you say their names?

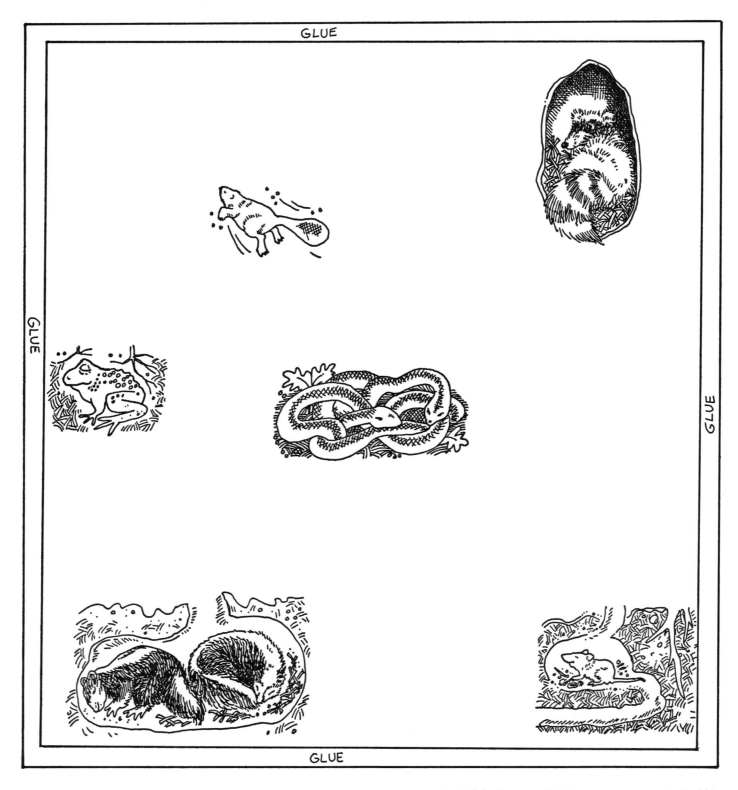

The Great Chase

Magnets are one of the wonders of the earth.

Each magnet has a north pole end and a south pole end.

Opposite poles ATTRACT each other.
They pull together in the same direction.

Poles that are the same REPEL.
They push each other apart.

You can use Casey Cat and Muffy Mouse to demonstrate
how magnets work.

Color and cut out Casey and Muffy.
Bend the tabs at the dotted lines and tape each animal to
a tiny bar magnet.

Place Casey and Muffy on a piece of cardboard.
Move a big nail underneath the board to make a cat-and-
mouse chase.

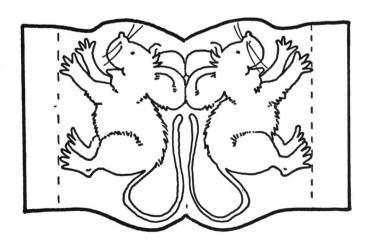

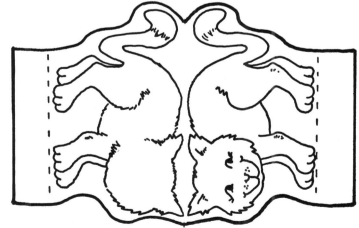

Can you make Casey and Muffy be friends and kiss each
other?

Tiny Treasures

Collect the very special treasures you can find tucked away in the secret places of the earth.

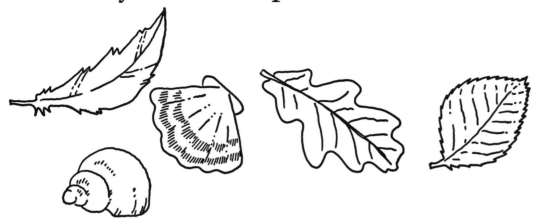

If you look carefully, you can find . . .

clover	seeds	stones	twigs	cones	burrs
moss	shells	rocks	pods	buds	feathers
grasses	nuts	pebbles	flowers	fossils	bark
sand	gravel	leaves	insects	weeds	old nests

You can carry your treasures in tiny jars, bags, cans, or boxes. See how many different sizes, shapes, and colors you can collect.

Be sure not to touch berries you don't know. Some are poison!

Don't take nests or animal homes that are still in use! You don't want to be a robber!

Make collages on large pieces of construction paper or classify and store your treasures in special containers.

Can you name all the treasures you have found?

Wash your hands with warm, soapy water when you finish collecting.

Celebrate!

(Two Body Dramas about the Seasons and Earth and Sky)

CELEBRATE THE SEASONS
(may be spoken or sung to the tune of "Twinkle, Twinkle, Little Star")

Winter, *(Hug yourself and shiver.)*
Summer, *(Shade your eyes.)*
Spring, *(Wiggle fingers to imitate rain.)*
And Fall. *(Make hands wave like falling leaves.)*
We will
Celebrate *(Clap hands and turn body around.)*
Them all!

CELEBRATE EARTH AND SKY
(may be spoken or sung to the tune of "Skip To My Lou")

Sunbeams shining, oh so bright,
(Raise arms over head in large circular motions.)
Fluffy clouds so fat and white,
(Make large circular motions around body.)
Stars that twinkle in the night,
(Wiggle fingers high in the air.)
High, high, high above us!
(Look up and point to the sky.)

Grasses green and earth so brown,
(Make swaying motion with hands, then squat and pat earth.)
Plants and flowers in the ground,
(Pretend to pick flowers.)
Friendly creatures all around.
(Mimic movements of animals.)

All on the earth to love us.
(Fold hands across chest to signify love.)

YOU CAN BE A LABORATORY SCIENTIST!

A laboratory scientist experiments to find answers.

NICE ICE SHAPES

Fill a variety of containers with water and freeze:
- shallow round pans (to make pancake shapes)
- cylinders and tin tubes (to make tall shapes)
- balloons (to make round shapes)
- ice-cube trays and muffin tins (to make small shapes)
- cake or gelatin molds (to make doughnut shapes)

Experiment to see which shapes melt the fastest.
How does each shape float?

More Experiments With Ice

Which is the fastest way to melt an ice cube?
Experiment to see.

Hold it in your hand.
Place it in the sun.
Place it on a light-colored surface.
Place it on a dark-colored surface.

Can you think of other ways?

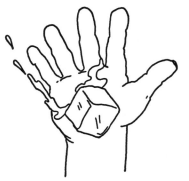

Which is the best ice cube keeper?

A cloth or towel?
A cardboard box?
An egg carton?
A pile of sand?
A pile of sawdust?

Experiment to see!

Making Waves

Find a glass jar with a good, tight-fitting screw top.
Fill the jar a little less than half full with white vinegar.
Finish filling the jar almost to the top with cooking oil.

Screw on the top and gently roll the jar back and forth to create tiny, ocean-like waves.
Add a paper raft or boat, if you wish.
Tell what you think makes the waves.

Maybe you can make up an ocean song to sing while you are watching the waves.

The Big Blow

Set two big, heavy books on their ends, like this.
Fill your cheeks with air and try to blow the books down.
Can you?

Now set the books close together.
Blow up a balloon between the books.

Uh, oh—Look what happens!
So, you really can blow down a heavy book with air!

Run With The Wind!

- Color both sides of the pinwheel.
- Cut the square on the straight, solid lines, but DO NOT CUT into the small center circle!
- Find each corner that has a dot. (There are 4.)
- Bend the paper and glue each dot to the center circle of the pinwheel.
- Poke a straight pin through the center circle and the four glued corners to attach the pin to the eraser of a pencil.

- Blow on your pinwheel OR
- Hold it high over your head and run into the wind.

Puff Darts

Get some drinking straws that are wrapped in paper.

Tear the wrapper at one end and carefully remove it from the straw.
Cut the wrapper in two.
Twist one end of the wrapper shut and slip it back on the straw.

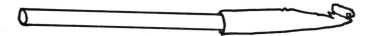

To shoot the dart, blow a hard quick puff of air through the straw.
Make a round cardboard target and try to hit the middle of the circle.

What makes your darts work?
Wind is moving air. You are a wind machine!

Hard Work Made Easy

Fill a cardboard box with books or blocks.
Push the box across the floor.

Now, place the box on a wagon or something that has wheels.
Is it easier to move?

Ask someone older to carry the box to a playground slide.
Set the box on the slide and push it down.
Does the slide make it easier to move the box?

The slide and the wheels are simple machines.
They help to make work easier.

Touch each machine picture and tell how it may make a person's job easier.

Which machines might a carpenter use?
Which might make it easier to clean a house?

Which machines are usually found in a kitchen?
Which are used mostly for fun?

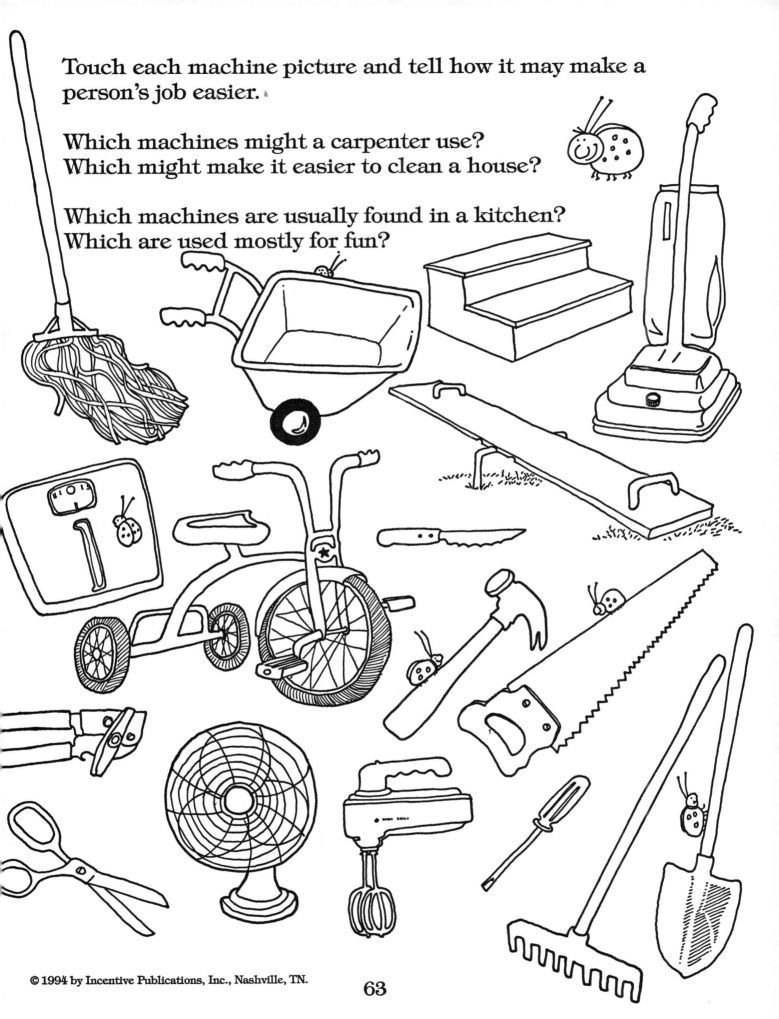

Glass Magic

Amaze your friends!

1. Stuff a paper napkin into the bottom of a small glass.

2. Fill a mixing bowl with water deep enough to cover the glass.

3. Turn the glass upside-down, and put it straight down into the water. (Don't tip it to the side.)

4. Then pull it straight up out of the water.

5. Touch the napkin. How did it stay dry?

The glass was full of air. The air in the glass pushed against the water. There was no room in the glass for water.

Now, do the trick again. This time, tip the glass a little as you put it in the water. WHOOPS! What happens?

Sound Box

Find a small cardboard box and several rubber bands of different thicknesses.

Stretch the rubber bands around the box as shown. (You can keep them in place by making notches.)

Pluck each band and listen to the sound it makes.
Which bands make higher sounds?
Which make lower sounds?
Why?

What Does Your Salt Garden Grow?

Salt . . . of course!

Find some porous stones or pieces of charcoal.
Fill a bowl about half full with water.
Keep adding salt and stirring until no more salt will
dissolve in the water.
Then stir in a tablespoon of vinegar.

Now fill the bowl of
salty water with
the stones you have
collected.

In one day, the salt
crystals will begin
to "grow" and your
bowl of stones will
begin to look like a
"magic" castle.

YOU CAN BE A SCIENCE DETECTIVE!

A detective investigates to solve problems.

THE SILLY ANIMAL SONG

Listen to each rhyme and guess the name of the animal.
Then act out the rhyme.

Silly animal, number ONE—
How you waddle when you run. *(Waddle.)*
Beak in front and tail in back, *(Move hand to mouth to imitate beak,*
hand at back to imitate tail.)
You waddle while you quack-quack-quack. *(Waddle and quack.)*

Silly animal, number TWO—
Hippity, hoppity, how-do-you-do? *(Hop, shake hands.)*
Hopping forward, hopping back, *(Hop forward, then back.)*
Baby riding in your sack. *(Hold arms out in front, hands clasped.)*

Silly animal, number THREE—
Swimming, swimming in the sea, *(Swim.)*
Diving in and leaping out, *(Dive and leap.)*
Blowing water through your spout. *(Hold hands overhead to imitate*
water spouting.)

Silly animal, number FOUR—
Practicing your frightful roar. *(Cover ears.)*
Your teeth can make an awful crunch *(Use hands to mimic large teeth*
crunching.)
I don't want to be your lunch! *(Shake head "no.")*

Silly animal, number FIVE—
Busy buzzing 'round your hive, *(Wiggle fingers by ears.)*
I will use a spoon to eat *(Make eating motions.)*
Your golden honey—sticky, sweet.

So You Want To Be A Scientist!

How do scientists find answers to big questions?
They read . . . they observe . . . they experiment . . .
they think . . . they listen . . . they talk with each other.
They discuss ideas with people who are older or wiser
than they are!
They use books, computers, cameras, and many kinds of
scientific instruments.

Here are some tricky questions that older scientists have
already answered. See if you can use your scientific skills
to learn what they have discovered.

What causes lightning?

What causes allergies?

How do wild geese find their way south?

What causes a shooting star?

How do zebras get their stripes?

How many years does it take a giant oak to grow from a tiny acorn?

You didn't let those tricky pictures fool you, did you?

How does the ocean know where to stop on the sand?

Time Changes Things

Scientists are careful observers.
They watch for important changes in our world.

Use your scientist's eyes to look at the changes shown in these pictures.
Can you explain the changes you see?

Circle the objects below that will change QUICKLY with time.
Tell how each will change.
Put an X on the ones that you think will change VERY SLOWLY.
Why will their change be so slow?

My Name Is _____

Guess What!

When scientists look for answers, they gather all the information possible.
Then they guess what the answer might be.

You can practice guessing as a scientist does by playing this game with your friends.
Find 5 or 6 objects in your house or classroom that may be identified by using one or more of your senses.

Put each in a box and wrap it like a present. Make a tiny picture of what is in each box and tape it on the bottom of the box.

Ask your friends to guess what is in each box by using all their senses.

They may feel the box, smell the box, shake the box, and listen to the contents move.

When they have made a guess, let them look at the picture taped to the bottom of the box to check their guesses.
Then they may open the box to see.

Scavenger Hunt

Scientists are good investigators. They think and act carefully and quickly. This game will sharpen the skills you need to be a good scientist.

See how quickly you can find . . .

   . . . something that tastes sweet.

   . . . something changed by the sun or rain.

   . . . something green, something brown, and something yellow.

   . . . a simple machine.

   . . . an animal that would fit on a teaspoon.

   . . . something that smells pleasant.

   . . . something that is older than you are.

   . . . something that is soft and fluffy.

   . . . something made by an animal.

   . . . something that changes shape or color when the temperature changes.

   . . . something that pollutes the earth.

A Rainbow
On Your Ceiling

If the sun is shining, there could be a rainbow on your ceiling. And you wouldn't even know it!

See if you can find it by following these directions:
- Place a small mirror in a clear glass filled with water.
- Find a place where the sun is shining.
- Place the glass so that the sun shines on the mirror.
- Then turn the glass slowly until a rainbow is reflected against a wall or ceiling.

Where do the colors come from?
How can you find out?

Just For Fun . . .
A Silly Card Trick

Do you think your body can pass through the center of the card at the bottom of this page?

Try this to see:
- Cut on the outside edges to remove the card from this page.
- Fold the card lengthwise, down the middle.
- Cut it, as shown, on the solid lines.
- Open the card and cut on the center fold line, just to the Xs.
- Spread the parts of the card to make a ring large enough to step into and pass up and over your head!
- Yea! You did it!

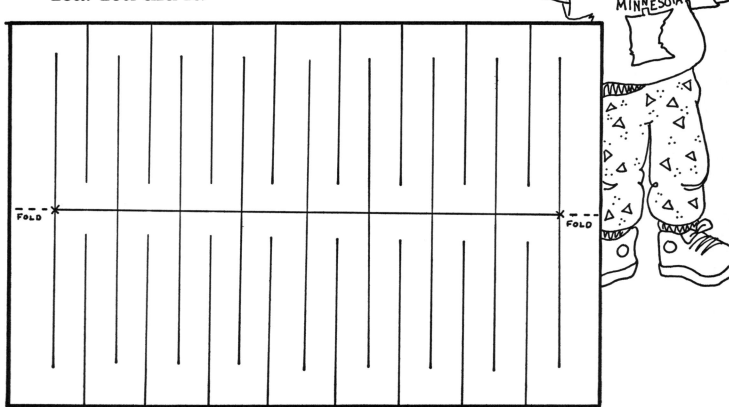

A scientific thinker can understand things that many people cannot understand.

Creative Insects

Reinforce the concept that insects have three main body parts and six legs while establishing a readiness for further exploration of insects by helping children create their very own ladybugs.

- Provide egg carton sections, construction paper, scissors, red and black tempera paint, paintbrushes, and paste. Help the children each cut six construction paper strips for legs. (For younger or less mature children, provide pre-cut strips.) Egg carton sections may be painted red with black spots. Heads can be painted on the egg carton sections, and the leg strips can be pasted on.

- Use the following recipe to make "art dough" for children to use to shape insects of their own design.

Art Dough

2 cups flour	4 tsp. cream of tartar
1 cup salt	2 cups water, with food coloring
2 tbs. oil	

Heat mixture, stirring until it forms a clump of dough.

- Help children make "Blob Paint Insects." Have them fold their painted papers in half, cut out butterfly shapes, and attach pipe cleaners for antennae.

Five Bees

Young children never tire of fingerplays. Here's a good one to use to introduce a study of bees. A "tasting party" complete with a taste of honeycomb would make a good follow-up activity.

> Here is the beehive. *(Clench fist.)*
> Where are the bees?
> Hiding away where nobody sees.
> Look! They are coming out. *(Loosen fist.)*
> They are all alive!
> One! Two! Three! Four! Five! *(Extend one finger at a time.)*

Animal Antics

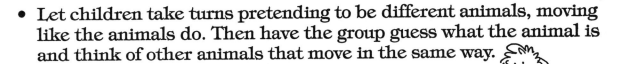

- Let children take turns pretending to be different animals, moving like the animals do. Then have the group guess what the animal is and think of other animals that move in the same way.

- Cut simple outline pictures of animals from coloring books (or draw your own). Cut pictures in half and paste each half on a piece of manila paper. Let children draw the other half of the animal.

- A super-easy insect cage may be made by cutting off the bottom of a liter-size bottle and covering it with an old nylon stocking. Make a class chart to record the story of the insects.

- Make an earthworm farm. Use layers of different types of soil (sand, red soil, black humus, etc.) so that children can tell how the worm works its way through the soil.

- Fold a piece of posterboard in half; glue a farm scene on one half and a zoo scene on the other. Provide plastic animals for children to classify by placing in the appropriate sections.

- Insect Safari: Make a wire ring from a coat hanger. Put it on the ground and direct children to check the "trap" for living creatures. Provide magnifying glasses so that children can examine their "catch."

Plant Participation

- Bring in plants or vegetables with very obvious roots (carrot, onion, turnip, spider plant, etc.) and let children determine which roots we eat. Then stage a tasting party!

- Read or tell the story of Johnny Appleseed. Cut an apple horizontally and show children the "star" shape in the core. Discuss how apples grow from seeds. Draw or paint pictures to show the process.

- Examine a pumpkin, discuss how it grows, and cut it open to explore the "insides." Plant a pumpkin seed to watch it grow. Then make a pumpkin seed snack:

  > 2 cups pumpkin seeds
  > 1 tbs. melted butter
  > 1¼ tsp. salt
  > Bake at 250 degrees for one to two hours until light brown.

- Make applesauce or blender peanut butter. Ask children to make a class chart showing the steps.

- Read and act out *The Carrot Seed* by Ruth Krauss (Harper & Row). Children love the movement!

- Start a windowsill herb garden. Label the pots and watch the garden grow! Use the mature herbs in a lunch salad to which children contribute by bringing vegetables from home.

- Help children plant grass seeds in eggshell halves and draw faces on the shells.

An Out-of-Doors Feast

To heighten awareness of the natural environment, help the children create a make-believe out-of-doors feast. Look for shells, leaves, and stones for cups and dishes, a puddle for a sink, flat rocks for a stove, sticks for stirring, and any other lovely natural materials your space affords. Just for fun, involve the children in making up a fancy menu. Print it on a chart and enjoy sharing it with parents and other visitors.

Here's a sample menu:

menu

• APPETIZERS •

Flowers laid in fancy patterns on a bark or cardboard tray.

• GRAVEL SOUP •

A cup of rain water. Add a pinch of dust and 2 leaves for seasoning. Simmer slowly on a hot rock.

• MOSS SALAD •

Pull moss from sides of trees or rocks. Add grass and weed stems. Set on a large green leaf. Garnish with flower petals.

• SAND WICHES •

Spread mud or wet sand between leaves or bark.

• GRILLED DELIGHT •

Spread mud on large flat leaves and grill on a hot rock until dry.

• SPAGHETTI SUPREME •

Two handfuls of dandelion stems or onion grass. Add minced grass for seasoning, + sprinkle grated dirt on top.

• UPSIDE-DOWN CAKE •

Spread layer of pine needles in pan. Pour whipped mud and spread. Bake in sun and turn upside-down.

• RAINSPOUT TEA •

Serve with a twist of squashed berry in acorn cups.

Of course, you will want to remember to take along a "For Real Feast" for your young explorers to enjoy. If possible, try to plan this as an excursion to a park, riverbank, or woodland area and hope for a lovely day on which kites can be flown, rocks and a stream explored, and insects chased and discussed. What a super way to explore nature in a manner sure to make a lasting impression on your young scientists!

Hands-On Science

- Set aside space for a "Look Nook" in the classroom with nature or science objects. Change these items frequently.

- Prepare a nature bulletin board. Add real leaves, nuts, pine cones, or other seasonal items to a tree painted by the children. Ask the children to draw or paint pictures showing how the tree will change with the seasons.

- Place a large box decorated with natural scenes in a corner of the classroom for a private place. Make an "Occupied" sign for children to use to insure privacy.

- Throw a "paper plate dinner"! Have children cut from magazines pictures of nutritious meal items and paste them on paper plates.

- Kids love to make food prints out of shapes cut into potato halves, carrots, oranges, or celery. Provide paint or ink pads into which children can dip the vegetables, and paper to print on.

- Pour soda into vinegar and direct children to watch for the chemical reaction.

- Help children make pinwheels in bright, happy colors to take outside on a windy day. Read *Gilberto and the Wind* by Marie H. Ets (Viking Press).

- Weigh and measure all of the children at the beginning of the year and again at the end of the year. Record measurements from both times on a chart so that children can make comparisons to see how much they have grown.

- Make an inclined plane by placing a long block on the edge of a shelf. Use it as a ramp for toy cars. Read *Mike Mulligan and His Steam Shovel* by Virginia Lee Burton (Houghton Mifflin).

- Make a display of simple machines and label them. Ask children to sort by kind.

- Place ice cubes in an electric skillet to make steam. Then do an experiment to see if ice will float. Read *The Snowy Day* by Ezra Jack Keats (Viking Press).

- Use a thermometer to check the temperature in the room. Then put the thermometer on the windowsill to measure the temperature outside. Have children draw two thermometers and make a red line for the temperature on each. (Don't worry about accuracy.) It's more fun to do this in the winter so that a marked difference can be noted.

- Help children make "magic" winter pictures. Dissolve Epsom salts in warm water, and let children brush this mixture over their crayon winter pictures (white crayon on light blue paper gives a nice effect). The finished pictures will look frosted!

  Each child can also make a spring picture by painting a brown branch on colored construction paper and making white fingerprints along the branch for a "pussy willow effect."

- In a large area, make a trail for children to follow. Use chairs, tables, boxes, etc. Put a simple sign or symbol on each to give children experience in following directions. Incorporate the use of directions including left, right, over, under, etc.